FRESHMEN

^{TM}

Conception
Adolescence
Mother/Father
Love/Divorce
Skinny/Fat
Pretty/Ugly
Cool/Nerd
Social Conditioning
Childhood trauma
Pre School
Grade School
High School
College
Long distance relationship
Detention
Summer School

Cast out of the main dorms and forced to live in temporary housing in the Boughl Science Buidling, 14 members of the freshmen class of Freese College have been imbued with miraculous superpowers by the explosion of a mysterious device called the Ax-Cell-Erator!

With powers based on whatever they were thinking at that pivotal moment, some of the kids are blessed with fantastic abilities, like the power to seduce others, or tandem telekinesis. But others are cursed: A die-hard vegan can communicate with plants and vegetables, leaving him nothing to eat. A math whiz must become drunk or stoned in order to inebriate his enemies. One kid woke up with a major boost to his... personal equipment. And then there's a talking Beaver with a major attitude.

Led by a lifelong comic book fan who missed the life-changing event, the kids have to deal with the everyday trials of college while learning to become superheroes and delving into the mystery of their superpowered rival fraternity.

Calculus
Foreign Language
Music
Science
Engineering

MAD...
SIMPLY
MAD.

Kegger

Freak Superpower inducing accident
Good vs. Evil
Secret Headquaters   Henchmen
Mask vs. No Mask
Cape vs Cape and Cowl
Social Responsibility
Time Travel   Grade
Vigilante
Public service announcements
Graduate
Licensing Codenames
Diploma
Career

FRESHMEN

Date Due

APR 10
3/1

Freshmen

co-created by
Seth Green
and **Hugh Sterbakov**

written by
Hugh Sterbakov
pencils by
Leonard Kirk
inks by
Andrew Pepoy
colors by
Tyson Wengler
with additional colors by Blond
letters by
Troy Peteri

for even more info than that check out
www.freshmencomic.com
and
www.fatboughl.com

for Top Cow Productions, Inc.:

Marc Silvestri - CEO
Matt Hawkins - President and COO
Filip Sablik - Publisher
Rob Levin - VP - Editorial
Mel Caylo - VP - Marketing & Sales
Chaz Riggs - Graphic Design
Phil Smith - Managing Editor
Joshua Cozine - Assistant Editor
Alyssa Phung - Controller
Adrian Nicita - Webmaster
Scott Newman - Production Assistant

Hi3515

for this edition
Book Design and Layout by:
Phil Smith

BK. 3

What did you think of this book?
We love to hear from our readers.

write us at:
fanmail@topcowent.com

**FREESE UNIVERSITY
COUNTY PUBLIC LIBRARY**

To find the comics shop nearest you call 1-888-COMICBOOK

for Image Comics
*publisher **Erik Larsen***
*executive director **Eric Stephenson***

Freshmen™ vol. 1 trade paperback, March 2008. SECOND PRINTING.
ISBN: 978-1-58240-593-3

TABLE OF CONTENTS:

Well, here it is, kids! The wait is over. You can read it all in one sit-ting and you don't have to extract the individual issues from their UV protective clamshell cases, locked deep in the temperature controlled basement in your folks' home.

When Hugh and I first set out to make this comic, I never expected people to have such intense reactions. Thank you so much to everyone that's read and supported this book- it means a lot to us.

A special thanks is owed to Jim and Matt for your enormous support and enthusiasm. You really let us do what we wanted, and gave us the best ingredients available. Big ups to Leonard Kirk, who deserves credit for helping to define the look of the characters. Leonard, the subtleties of your drawings really capture the complexities of our kids' personality. To Andrew, Joe Linsner, and of course, Rodolfo- we're nothing without you. This has been an incredible experience, and we're thrilled to share it with you.

The story is a simple one, of young kids on their own for the first time in their lives. Meant to discover themselves and cement the identities that they will embody for the rest of their lives...with super powers. It's a story about whom you choose to befriend, whom you trust to love, how you define yourself and where your loyalties lay.

So what are you waiting for? Turn the page and get to know our kids! Great adventures await...

Seth Green

February 2006

You've never heard of me before Freshmen. That's okay. I'm the guy who just took the most fulfilling crap in history.

I grew up with an unquenchable thirst for comics. I learned to read on Gerry Conway's Spider-Man run and I came of age under the thrall of Stan Lee, Roger Stern, Matt Wagner, Chris Claremont, Peter David, Alan Moore, Frank Miller and Denny O'Neil. I was that little punk 13 year-old that terrorized every comic convention and store near Philadelphia, and soon enough I started creating my own comics. I was thrown out of so many high school classes for doodling that I nearly didn't graduate.

Then I spent 10 grueling years in the Hollywood development grind. It took away my dignity, my self-esteem, my sense of justice and my hair. But in comics, there's no soulwrenching bottleneck between your imagination and your audience. You write it, they draw it, somebody eventually reads it. And so, having real people read this story was my laxative for the world's wickedest bout of constipation. Yep, I just took a giant metaphoric crap all over the comic book industry and you're holding it in your hands. Unless I've talked you out of it, you're about to read it.

Not that these comics are crap—I couldn't be more pleased than offering Freshmen as my breakout work. It represents me well, since I am every one of these characters at different times of the day. They're confused, unsure, angry, overburdened and neurotic. They're prone to flights of fancy or brutal self-loathing. They're desperate to speak their minds, but terrified of not fitting in. They've become so familiar to me that they write themselves now—I almost feel guilty taking credit for them. But, like I said, I've been hard up. So I will.

When I finished writing this series, I felt like I'd made a bunch of new friends in these characters. I hope you feel the same. Thanks for sharing this crap with me, folks. Read on—it can only get better from here.

Hugh Sterbakov
February 1, 2006

I JUST WATCHED THEM FOR A COUPLE MINUTES--EVERY CREED, EVERY COLOR, AND WONDERED WHERE I'D FIT IN. DIDN'T SEEM LIKE ANYONE ELSE WAS NERVOUS.

THERE ARE A LOT OF FIRST STEPS YOU HAVE TO TAKE IN LIFE, AND I GUESS YOU NEVER KNOW EXACTLY WHERE THEY'RE GOING TO LEAD.

THIS, FOR EXAMPLE, WAS MY FIRST STEP TOWARD BECOMING A SUPERHERO.

SUPERHERO BASICS 101:
INTRODUCTION TO
SUPER POWERS

WELCOME FRESHMEN!
D.W. FREESE WELCOMES OUR
NEXT GENERATION!

BOY, THEY KNOW HOW TO TAKE YOUR DIGNITY AWAY AT COLLEGE. REAL QUICK.

WE WERE STUFFED INTO A CLASSROOM IN THE SCIENCE BUILDING. FIVE GIRLS IN ONE ROOM. AND WE ALL MIGHT AS WELL BE FROM DIFFERENT UNIVERSES.

PAULA POPHOUSE, FROM NEW HAMPSHIRE, DEFINES THE FAN BASE OF US MAGAZINE: SHE LIVES FOR SOAPY, LOVESTRUCK GOSSIP. DIDN'T EXACTLY WIN THE GENETICS LOTTERY, THOUGH. I THINK THE BUBBLINESS MASKS A VERY TROUBLED GIRL.

RENEE BELLOCHIO, A JERSEY GIRL THROUGH AND THROUGH, COMPLETE WITH TEASED HAIR AND MAD BLING. YUP, I JUST WROTE "MAD BLING." SHE NODDED TO ME WHEN SHE WALKED IN. THAT MUST PASS FOR VALIDATION IN SKANKVILLE.

THEN THERE'S "CACOPHONY," OR SO SHE CALLS HERSELF, WHO SITS IN THE CORNER AND GLARES. AND I MEAN GLARES. SHE SHOULD BE IN THE GLARING OLYMPICS. WHO CAN SHE HATE THAT MUCH?

ONE GIRL HASN'T ARRIVED YET. I ALREADY LIKE HER BEST.

BOUGH SCIENCE BUILDING

I WAS IMPRESSED WITH THE COLLEGE WORK-LOAD COMPARED TO HIGH SCHOOL. THERE'S CLEARLY A LOT MORE RESPONSIBILITY DEMANDED OF US, AND FAR LESS ROOM FOR EXCUSES. NO CHALLENGING SUBJECTS JUST YET, BUT THEY WERE HANDHOLDING THE FRESHMEN AND I COULDN'T BLAME THEM.

I *REALLY* COULDN'T BLAME THEM.

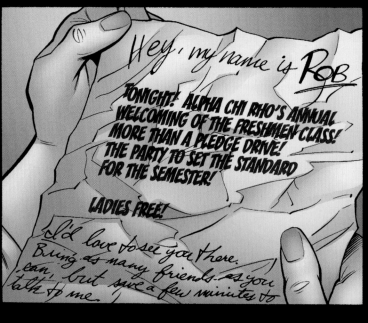

Hey, my name is ROB

TONIGHT! ALPHA CHI RHO'S ANNUAL WELCOMING OF THE FRESHMEN CLASS! MORE THAN A PLEDGE DRIVE! THE PARTY TO SET THE STANDARD FOR THE SEMESTER!

LADIES FREE!

I'd love to see you there. Bring as many friends as you can, but save a few minutes to talk to me.

OKAY. I'D REALLY LIKE TO TELL YOU THAT I WAS DISGUSTED BY THIS CHILDISH DISPLAY AND INSULTED BY THE CHAUVINISTIC INVITATION.

BUT... DAMMIT.

THAT BOY WAS CUTE.

A SPLIT-SECOND IN TIME. A MOMENT WHICH, UNDER NORMAL CIRCUMSTANCES, YOU'D LIKELY NEVER PAY A SECOND THOUGHT.

HOLY BIBLE

PASSING THROUGH THE RITES OF ADOLESCENCE.

GEEZ... I'VE NEVER HAD A BEER BEFORE.

WELCOME FRESH PEEPS!

DEALING WITH REJECTION.

ANYBODY HUNGRY?

I'M GOING TO GET A PIZZA.

CLINGING TO FAMILIARITY.

YES, YOU'LL GROW BIG AND STRONG, BABY. YOU'RE SAFE WITH ME, SUSIE, I'LL ALWAYS LOVE YOU.

COLD IN 'ERE...?

AFRAID TO LET GO.

OH, BABY...

TRYING TO FIT IN.

YES! I DID IT! ALL 600 POST-ITS!

ABOUT TO BE THRUST INTO ADULTHOOD.

READY OR NOT.

HAVE A FUN YEAR!

NEXT ISSUE: COSTUMES!

LIAM? I CAN MAKE THE GROUND RUMBLE THROUGH VIBRATIONS IN MY STOMACH!

CHARLES? I CAN...HEAR...PLANTS. THEY TALK TO ME.

VERY WELL THEN.

THEY WON'T STOP. MAKE THEM STOP.

JIMMY?

uhm...KIND OF OBVIOUS? THINGS ARE, LIKE, STICKING TO ME. LIKE... EVERYTHING. EVERYTHING IS F*BLEEEP*S STICKING TO ME.

I CAN JUMP INTO OTHER PEOPLE'S MINDS. LOOK AROUND, VIEW THEIR MEMORIES, INTERPRET THEIR THOUGHTS...EVEN CONTROL THEM A LITTLE.

FASCINATING, ANNALEE. VERY GOOD THEN. AND JACQUES?

I...DO NOT KNOW. I CAN ONLY SAY ZAT...THINGS 'AVE BEEN...ODD.

ALRIGHT, THEN. RAY?

uhm...I'VE BEEN...ENHANCED. HUGE. GIGANTIC. Y'KNOW...HUNG LIKE A HORSE? EXCEPT THIS IS MORE LIKE A GARDEN HOSE.

er...VERY GOOD THEN. ELWOOD?

Hunh? SHHHH.

HE CAN BURP AT PEOPLE AND MAKE THEM DRUNK.

NO, YOU CAN! YOU'RE DRUNK!

NORRIN? HAVE YOU ANY INTERESTING NEW ABILITIES?

YOU CAN PASS RIGHT BY ME. I GOT NOTHIN'. I MISSED IT. I WENT FOR PIZZA.

MAN. PIZZA.

I'M SORRY, NORRIN. I DON'T THINK I HAVE ANY POWERS EITHER, IF IT MAKES YOU FEEL ANY BETTER.

OR HUNG OVER. I C'N MAKE YA HUNG OVER TOO. I SAID THAT. WAIT, WHAT'U YOU SAY?

IT TOOK PAULA A WHILE TO DISCOVER HER POWERS.

IT MADE PERFECT SENSE, THOUGH: A DIE-HARD ROMANTIC WHO'D NEVER HAD SO MUCH AS A SINGLE DATE IN HER LIFE GAINS THE ABILITY TO MAKE ANYONE FALL IN LOVE WITH HER.

SHE CAN TURN UTTER DEVOTION ON OR OFF LIKE A SPIGOT. I THINK THAT'S IRONIC. BUT, HONESTLY, I CAN NEVER FIGURE OUT WHAT IRONIC REALLY MEANS.

WHAT'S UP? HAVE WE MET?

uhm... NO?

no, really, it's way better to be crushed than burned. you made my day. I'm stoked. let's party.

WELL, LET ME CORRECT THAT IMMEDIATELY, GIRL, 'CAUSE YOU HAVE GOT IT GOIN' ON! WHAT'S YOUR STORY, YOU WANNA KICK IT LATER?

HEY, LOVER BOY...

31

...OF NORRIN WEISMEYER. STARDATE: SEPTEMBER 5. THE TEAM HAS INFILTRATED JOMITA STADIUM AT WATSON UNIVERSITY. IT'S THEIR HOMECOMING FOOTBALL GAME, AGAINST OUR OWN FREESE BEAVERS.

ONE BOTTLE DOWN.

NEXT ONE'S UP. HOW YA FEELIN', ELWOOD?

WEEE.

BUUUURP!

WHAT THE--

OOOOO!

OKAY, PAULA, YOU STAY HERE, TAKE CARE OF HIM. ANYBODY ASKS YOU TO MOVE, THEY FALL IN LOVE WITH YOU.

YES SIR!

EVERYONE ELSE, FOLLOW NORRIN.

HOO-BOY... I GOT A BEAUT BREWIN'.

LET ME 'ELP YOU.

YOUR COSTUME IS VERY BECOMING, MY DEAR. VERY SEXY.

BRRRRUUUGH!

HEE HEE...

WHATSH DIS? HEE HEE... HELLO MISTER FOOTBALL.

HURKKK--

LET'S HIT IT, GUYS. WE GOT THE ITEM.

GREAT!

HEY, ANNALEE--

-- ISN'T THAT ROB, FROM THE FRAT PARTY?

DEAR MUM (WITH FOND HELLOS TO AMY, ADAM, JOHN, LITTLE MARY AND ESPECIALLY PA, GRAMPS AND ME-MOM)...

I'M SORRY IT'S BEEN SO LONG SINCE I'VE WRITTEN. THERE ARE MANY THINGS I'VE WISHED TO SHARE WITH YOU ALL, BUT I HAD TO WAIT UNTIL THE PROPER TIME.

NOW I CAN FINALLY TELL YOU THE WHOLE STORY.

YOU SEE, MY NEW COLLEGE FRIENDS AND I HAVE BECOME SUPERHEROES.

FRESHMEN

SUPERHERO BASICS 103: SUPERVILLAIN COMPREHENSION

HELLO...? SOMEONE OUT THERE?

I'VE FOUND MANY MORE AMAZING MACHINES SINCE I LAST WROTE. MY ROOMMATE HAS AN ELECTRIC TOOTHBRUSH. AND THERE ARE ALSO ELECTRICAL RAZORS, BLANKETS AND PENCIL SHARPENERS. THEY ARE ALL REALLY VERY HANDY.

ONE MACHINE, HOWEVER, CALLED THE AX-CELL-ERATOR, IS THE MOST AMAZING OF ALL. IT WAS DESIGNED BY ONE OF THE SCHOOL'S PROFESSORS, AND IT'S GOING TO TEACH LIVING CELLS TO FIX THEMSELVES, CURING DISEASE AND POSSIBLY EVEN AGING.

IT EXPLODED A WEEK INTO THE SEMESTER. THAT'S HOW WE GOT OUR SUPERPOWERS.

SUPERPOWERS, MUM! IF YOU COULD CALL THEM THAT. THEY'RE SORT OF WEIRD, NOT WHAT YOU'D USUALLY SEE IN THE MOVING PICTURES.

BELLLLLCH

OhGod OhGod OhGod OhGod OhGod...

MY FRIEND ELWOOD, WHO WE CALL THE INTOXICATOR, CAN BURP AT ANYONE AND MAKE THEM DRUNK. OR HUNG OVER. BASICALLY, HOWEVER HE'S FEELING AT THE TIME.

OF COURSE, ALCOHOL IS NOT VIRTUOUS, MUM. HOWEVER, ELWOOD ALWAYS USES HIS POWER FOR THE GOOD OF THE COMMUNITY.

RRRGGGKK HURRRRRP!

WE'RE TRYING TO BECOME A TEAM.

...BUT NOT FOLLOWING THROUGH WITH THEIR HEARTS.

THE BIBLE SAYS PRIDE IS A SIN.

THE AMISH DRESS VERY PLAIN SO AS NOT TO APPEAR PROUD. DIDN'T YOU EVER SEE WITNESS?

NOW WHY YOU GONNA WEAR THAT ON THE INSIDE OF YOUR HAT?

BUT THEY DO IT WRONG, MUM, LIKE EVERYTHING ELSE. CLAIMING ON THE OUTSIDE TO BE ONE THING...

WHATNESS?

WE NEED TO DECIDE WHAT THE "F" STANDS FOR. COME UP WITH OUR SUPERHERO TEAM NAME.

WHAT ABOUT FREESE FORCE FIVE?

AWWW... HOW CUTE. DOES FREESE FORCE FIVE WEAR MAN-DRESSES AND HIGH HEELS?

HOW ABOUT DUMB *BLEEP* *BLEEP* WADS FROM *BLEEP* VILLE? HUH? THAT WORK FOR YOU?

SOUNDS ABOUT RIGHT, WITH YOU ON THE TEAM.

LISTEN, *BLEEP*, I'M GETTI[N] TIRED OF YOU NAGGING ME, YOU HEAR? YOU'[R]E DROP YOUR *BLEEP* LIKE LA[ST] POTATO. YOU KNOW [WHAT,] KNOW WHAT-- YO[U] EVEN DESERV[E] YOU DON'T DESERV[E] HOW I TREAT YOU. [I] DON'T EVER TALK TO [YOU] *BLEEP* LIKE THAT? [T]REAT YOU WITH [RES]PECT, BUT THAT'S [I]T-- NO MORE.

BLEEP YOU, *BLEEP* YOUR ATTITUDE, AND *BLEEP* THE HORS[E] YOU RODE IN ON! NO, Y'KNOW WHAT, I BETTER NOT SAY THAT, 'CAUSE YOU'LL GO AND *BLEEP* THE [H]ORSE--

FRESHMEN.

WE'RE FRESHMEN. ANYBODY REMEMBER SCHOOL?

YOU SHOULDA STUCK WITH ME, ANNALEE, I'D HAVE TREATED YOU RIGHT.

HERE'S WHAT YOU GET FOR RUNNING WITH THE GEEKS!

AIN'T SO TOUGH, *BLEEP*.

THE VIOLENCE WAS SHOCKING.

THAT SO?

FWOOSH

WHEE! DO IT AGAIN, MOM!

WANNABE-- KENNETH "NORRIN" WEISMEYER, THE WOULD-BE TEAM LEADER--

--AND RESIDENT SUPERHERO GEEK, WHO WENT FOR PIZZA DURING THE PIVOTAL MOMENT AND HAS NO POWERS!

THE PUPPETEER-- ANNALEE ROGERS--

--WHO CAN JUMP INTO PEOPLE'S MINDS AND VIEW THEIR MEMORIES OR EVEN CONTROL THEM!

THE GREEN THUMB-- CHARLES LEVY--

-- A DEDICATED VEGETARIAN WHO CAN NOW COMMUNICATE WITH PLANTS, LEAVING HIM NOTHING TO EAT!

QUAKER-- LIAM ADAMS--

--THE AMISH BOY WHO CAN CAUSE EARTHQUAKES BY SHUFFLING HIS BELLY!

THE INTOXICATOR-- ELWOOD JOHNS--

--FORMER MATH GENIUS WHOSE DRUNKEN BURPS INTOXICATE ANYONE WHO SMELLS THEM!

THE DRAMA TWINS-- RENEE AND BRADY--

--BICKERING EXES WHO MUST BE IN CONTACT TO USE THEIR TELEKINESIS!

THE SQUIRREL-- JACQUES LALLEAUX--

--THE FRENCH EXCHANGE STUDENT WHO COMPULSIVELY HOARDS NUTS!

THE SEDUCTRESS-- PAULA POPHOUSE--

THE RELATIONSHIP-OBSESSED TEEN WHO CAN MAKE ANYONE FALL IN LOVE WITH HER!

THE BEAVER-- THE SCHOOL MASCOT--

--IMBUED WITH QUANTUM-BUSTING INTELLIGENCE, BUT CAN'T CONCENTRATE ON ANYTHING BUT BUILDING DAMS!

DR. THEODORE TOMLINSON-- THE SCIENCE PROFESSOR WHO CREATED THE AX-CELL-ERATOR!

HOW...

VERY...

DISTURBING.

PREVIOUSLY IN FRESHMEN:
AFTER DISCOVERING THEIR BIZARRE AND AMAZING POWERS, OUR YOUNG HEROES WERE EMPLOYED BY THE CREATOR OF THE AX-CELL-ERATOR, DR. TOMLINSON, TO HELP REPAIR THE MACHINE THAT COULD CURE ALL DISEASES AND EVEN PREVENT AGING.

WANNABE, SUPERHERO OBSESSED BUT POWERLESS, HAS TAKEN DUBIOUS LEADERSHIP OF THE TEAM, BUT MOST OF THE KIDS TURN TO HIS UNREQUITED LOVE, THE PUPPETEER, FOR GUIDANCE.

ALTHOUGH THE KIDS' FIRST FIELD ASSIGNMENT WENT WELL, THEIR NEXT ADVENTURE TOOK A DISASTROUS TURN FOR THE DIRE, WHEN THE INEXPLICABLY HULKING FRAT GUYS INTERCEPTED THEIR MISSION AND STOLE A PIECE OF THE AX-CELL-ERATOR FROM UNDER THEM. IN THE MELEE, THE SEDUCTRESS WAS CRITICALLY INJURED...

EVERYONE DEALS WITH TRAGEDY IN THEIR OWN WAY.

SOME BREAK DOWN.

SOME GO INTO DENIAL. UNABLE TO DEAL WITH THE LOSS.

SOMETHING WRONG?

SOMETHING IS...MISSING. I MUST RUMINATE FURTHER ON THE SUBJECT.

AIIIGHT, YO, COAST IS CLEAR. WE GOOD TO GO.

WHY DO *I* HAVE TO DO THIS?

TRUST ME, SON, IT'LL BE MUCH BETTER THAN GETTING SLOSHED ALL THE TIME. LESS AFTERSHOCK.

INDEED, ELWOOD. IN THE INTEREST OF EXPERIMENT, I'D LIKE TO SEE IF YOUR POWERS EXTEND TO OTHER ITERATIONS OF INTOXICATION.

AND THIS MIGHT BE A PREFERABLE METHOD BY WHICH YOU'LL DRAW AMMUNITION.

WORD.

WHAT TIME IS IT IN BUDAPEST--

YOU SEE--THE THING IS--I MEAN... I DON'T KNOW. I ENCOUNTER FREE-FLOWING WATER-- BE THEY RIVERS OR STREAMS--AND I JUST HAVE THIS *INTENSE* DESIRE TO *STOP* THEM. I DO DECLARE I *MUST* BUILD THAT DAM.

IT'S A MONOMANIA, QUITE FRANKLY.

MONO-*WHAT*-IA?

MEGAMANIA? THAT OLD ATARI GAME? YO, DAT *BLEEP* WAS DA BOMB.

YEAH, MY BROTHER HAD THAT! BUT I PREFERRED KABOOM.

KABOOM! I HAD THAT! THAT GAME WAS AWESOME! IT USED THE PADDLES!

OH, GOD, YEAH, BUT THE BEST PADDLE GAME HAD TO BE CIRCUS ATARI. 'MEMBER THAT SOUND?

DONK! DONK! DONK DONK!

WHAT IN ALL THE GRAND DESIGN ARE YOU TWO BABBLING ABOUT?

SHE'LL *BE* THERE.

THE DOCTORS ARE STILL RUNNING TESTS, THEY DON'T KNOW IF SHE'S BRAIN DEA--

DON'T SAY IT.

PLEASE JUST...

DON'T SAY IT.

I CAN'T FEEL MY JAW.

SHE HASN'T CALLED YET. MUST NOT BE ANY CHANGE WITH PAULA.

RENEE IS GONNA CALL?

YEAH.

WHAT?

I DIDN'T SAY ANYTHING.

IT'S ALL MY FAULT.

NO, IT'S NOT, LIAM.

DON'T SAY THAT, LIAM. IT'S NOT.

Ooo. Big drama.

WHAT TIME IS IT IN BUDAPEST?

OKAY...I KNOW WHAT YOU'RE THINKING. YOU'RE THINKING WHY THE HELL DO I STAY WITH HER EVEN THOUGH SHE'S AN ABUSIVE *BLEEP*. THE WAY SHE TALKS TO ME AND EVERYTHING.

YOU JUST HAVE TO UNDERSTAND, THOUGH-- THIS IS MY FIRST LOVE. MY FIRST KISS. MY FIRST... EVERYTHING. I'VE BEEN WITH HER SINCE 7TH GRADE, I DON'T KNOW ANY DIFFERENT.

AND YOU GUYS HAVE ONLY SEEN US AT OUR WORST. WE HAVE THESE AMAZING MOMENTS, WHERE SHE UNDERSTANDS ME BETTER THAN ANY ONE EVER HAS.

IT JUST FEELS LIKE... IT FEELS LIKE... LIKE SHE'S HOME, Y'KNOW? IT FEELS LIKE NOTHING WOULD BE THE SAME WITHOUT HER.

WE ALWAYS KEEP FIGHTING. I JUST... I CAN'T GET HER TO TREAT ME RIGHT. I CAN'T GET HER TO RESPECT ME. DON'T MATTER IF I SEND HER FLOWERS OR I CURSE HER OUT... I ALWAYS GET THE SAME.

EVERYONE DEALS WITH TRAGEDY IN THEIR OWN WAY.

SOME ARE ASHAMED, FRUSTRATED BY THEIR VULNERABILITIES.

THE STRONGEST NEMESIS OF THE HUMAN PSYCHE IS SHAME. HUMILIATION.

IT LEADS TO INHIBITION. SELF-PROTECTION. RISK AVERSION. FREEZES YOU DEAD MORE THAN ANY PHYSICAL HANDICAP.

JACQUES.

WHAT ARE YOU DOING HERE?

NOS'ZING.

WHY AREN'T YOU AT THE HOSPITAL?

I WEEL GO WHEN I AM READY.

WHAT'S IN YOUR DRESSER, JACQUES?

NOS'ZING.

IT KEEPS YOU FROM OPENING UP TO STRANGERS. ACCEPTING HELP. MAKING FRIENDS.

I COULD *MAKE* YOU OPEN IT.

WHOA. I'VE GOT ONE BREWING.

HOO-BOY, THIS IS GOING TO BE--

BARRRRRUUUUUGGGHHF!

EVERYONE DEALS WITH TRAGEDY IN THEIR OWN WAY.

SOME TRY TO BARGAIN. RAGE AGAINST THAT WHICH THEY CANNOT CONTROL.

WHAT ARE WE GOING TO DO ABOUT THE FRAT GUYS?

WE'RE GOING TO REGROUP.

WE'RE GOING TO GET PREPARED.

WE'RE GOING TO FIND OUT EVERYTHING ABOUT THEM. WHERE THEY GOT THOSE POWERS.

UNPREPARED TO ADMIT THEIR HELPLESSNESS.

AND THEN WE'RE GOING TO DESTROY THEM.

--THE HELL ARE YOU GUYS DOING?

WE SHOULDN'T DO THIS WITHOUT THE OTHERS. THIS ISN'T EXACTLY THE HEAVY ARTILLERY OF OUR GROUP. I'M USELESS WITHOUT BRADY.

WHICH IS *INCREDIBLY* SAD.

I JUST WANT TO LOOK AROUND. SEE IF THERE'RE ANY CLUES ABOUT HOW THEY GOT SO STRONG. WE WON'T ENGAGE THEM. LOOK, AM I THE TEAM LEADER OR NOT? YOU'RE SUPPOSED TO LISTEN TO ME, REMEMBER?

HAAHAAHA HAAHAAHAHA HAHA HAA... HAA HAA HAHA

I HAVE TO... I HAVE TO PEE...

ANNALEE SAID SO.

HOW CAN YOU BE LAUGHING AT A TIME LIKE THIS? DON'T YOU KNOW WHAT'S GOING ON?

ANNALEE, I WANT TO HAVE THIS CONVERSATION WITH YOU...BUT...I DESPERATELY HAVE TO PEE...

ALRIGHT.

FINE. BUT NO FIGHTING.

WOW. LOOKS LIKE THE *ELM STREET* HOUSE IN *DREAM WARRIORS*.

DO YOU INGEST YOUR GEEK ORALLY, OR IS THERE LIKE A SHOT YOU TAKE--?

I DON'T THINK WE SHOULD GO IN THERE, NORRIN.

WE HAVE TO TAKE A LOOK. WE HAVE TO FIND OUT WHAT HAPPENED TO THEM. WHERE THEY MIGHT'VE TAKEN THE ION EXCITER.

WHY?

BECAUSE THAT DEVICE COULD FIX THE AX-CELL-ERATOR AND CHANGE THE WORLD. CURE DISEASE, END SUFFERING. WITH SCIENCE FREE TO FOCUS ON OTHER THINGS, WE COULD COLONIZE THE UNIVERSE, OR... OR...INVENT TIME TRAVEL... OR EVEN CLONE DINOSAURS!

OR INVENT NEW FLAVORS OF LIP GLOSS.

YOU DON'T SAY. GUYS, I THINK WANNABE IS ONTO SOMETHING.

DON'T CALL THAT.

I WANT TO JUMP INTO PAULA'S HEAD. TRY TO CONVINCE HER TO WAKE UP, SEE WHAT'S GOING ON--

ANNALEE, THAT MIGHT BE INCREDIBLY DANGEROUS. WE DON'T KNOW ENOUGH ABOUT YOUR--

I'M WILLING TO TAKE THE RISK!

BUT I'M NOT. WE HAVE ONE MEMBER DOWN, AND I'M SIMPLY UNWILLING TO RISK A SECOND.

WE DON'T KNOW ENOUGH ABOUT YOUR POWERS. YOU COULD BECOME COMATOSE YOURSELF. OR, INDEED, WORSE.

I'M GOING TO ASK DOCTOR TOMLINSON.

UNFORTUNATELY, I'M AFRAID YOU WON'T FIND HIM. THE AX-CELL-ERATOR IS GONE AS WELL.

WHAT?!

INDEED. I'M BEGINNING TO FEAR THAT OUR TRUST IN DR. TOMLINSON WAS MISGUIDED.

HOW COULD YOU NOT TELL ME THIS?

I CHOSE TO LET YOU, AND THE OTHER OVERLY-EMOTIONAL MONGOLOIDS IN OUR GROUP, HANDLE ONE SETBACK AT A TIME.

WHAT ARE WE GOING TO DO?

I HAVEN'T YET FORMULATED OUR NEXT STEP. MY FOCUS HAS BEEN ON PAULA'S HEALTH.

ODIN'S BLOOD!

YEAH, I CAN SEE THAT. NOTHING BUT FOCUS HERE.

HAAHAAHAAHOOHAA

DON'T MAKE ME LAUGH-- I HAVE TO PEE SO BAD.

GOMEN NASAI... please...

LOOK-- A BONSAI TREE.

THIS MAY BE TOO MUCH OF A CHALLENGE FOR OUR YOUNG TEAM, ANNALEE.

HAAA HAAH HAHA HAHA

I DON'T BELIEVE WE'RE PREPARED TO TAKE ON THOSE GHASTLY FELLOWS IN THEIR CURRENT CONDITION.

ANNALEE... ANNALEE... I HAVE AN IDEA.

MAN, I'VE GOTTA PEE. OH, WAIT... WHAT WAS I GOING TO SAY?

OH YEAH!

WHAT TIME IS IT IN BUDAPEST?

KONNICHIWA! I SPEAK... LITTLE ENGLISH.

WHAT HAPPENED HERE?

INTOXICATED, THEY WERE, BY THEIR NEWFOUND POWER. ROB-SAN, THEIR LEADER, WAS DESPERATE FOR MORE.

WHERE DID THEY GET THEIR POWERS?

OKAY, HERE'S THE THING, ANNALEE...

PLEASE TELL ME YOU'VE GOT SOME POTATO CHIPS OR SOMETHING.

OH YES, PLEASE DO!

TEE HEE... HA HA HA...

HOO-BOY. BATHROOM.

OH, MY WORD. I OFTEN WONDER ABOUT THAT...

NO BATH IN THE BATHROOM... YOU DON'T REST IN THE RESTROOM...

WHAT THE HELL, MAN? WHO'S IN CHARGE HERE?

WHO PUT STAIRS IN THE BATHROOM?!

WHAT THE--

PLEASE, SIR, PLEASE-- JUST A BIT MORE...

WHO IS THAT?

YOU'VE HAD ENOUGH, LET'S GET THE BOOKS AND GO.

MORE, PLEASE!

PLEASE! PLEASE!

NOBODY...

NONE OF THESE STUPID MEAT WADS WILL LISTEN TO ME...

RIGHT HAND OUT.

LEFT HAND OUT. PALMS UP.

NOBODY WILL LISTEN...

NORRIN...

RIGHT HAND TO LEFT SHOULDER.

YOU GUYS... YOU'RE NEVER GONNA GUESS WHAT I JUST SAW.

LEFT HAND TO RIGHT SHOULDER.

WHAT WAS...

RIGHT HAND BEHIND HEAD. LEFT HAND BEHIND HEAD.

YOU GUYS... I TOTALLY JUST... MAN...

RIGHT HAND ON LEFT HIP. LEFT HAND ON RIGHT HIP.

I JUST... GOSH, MAN, I JUST SAW SOMETHING... AND I CAN'T...

RIGHT HAND ON RIGHT HIP. LEFT HAND ON LEFT HIP. LEFT HIP, JIMMY.

I CAN'T FOR THE LIFE OF ME REMEMBER WHAT IT WAS.

NOW WIGGLE AND JUMP!

WHAT TIME IS IT IN BUDAPEST?

...DOCTOR TOMLINSON WANTS TO TALK WITH YOU.

NEXT ISSUE: URAGIRU!

Freshmen Preview, Wizard World Philadelphia variant
art by: **Rodolfo Migliari** the pride of Argentina

WANNABE-- KENNETH "NORRIN" WEISMEYER, THE WOULD-BE TEAM LEADER-- --AND RESIDENT SUPERHERO GEEK, WHO WENT FOR PIZZA DURING THE PIVOTAL MOMENT AND HAS NO POWERS!

THE PUPPETEER-- ANNALEE ROGERS-- --WHO CAN JUMP INTO PEOPLE'S MINDS AND VIEW THEIR MEMORIES OR EVEN CONTROL THEM!

THE GREEN THUMB-- CHARLES LEVY-- -- A DEDICATED VEGETARIAN WHO CAN NOW COMMUNICATE WITH PLANTS, LEAVING HIM NOTHING TO EAT!

QUAKER-- LIAM ADAMS-- --THE AMISH BOY WHO CAN CAUSE EARTHQUAKES BY SHUFFLING HIS BELLY!

THE INTOXICATOR-- ELWOOD JOHNS-- --FORMER MATH GENIUS WHOSE DRUNKEN BURPS INTOXICATE ANYONE WHO SMELLS THEM!

THE DRAMA TWINS-- RENEE AND BRADY-- --BICKERING EXES WHO MUST BE IN CONTACT TO USE THEIR TELEKINESIS!

THE SQUIRREL-- JACQUES LALLEAUX-- --THE FRENCH EXCHANGE STUDENT WHO COMPULSIVELY HOARDS NUTS!

THE SEDUCTRESS-- PAULA POPHOUSE-- THE LOVELORN TEEN WHO CAN MAKE ANYONE FALL IN LOVE WITH HER!

THE BEAVER-- THE SCHOOL MASCOT-- --IMBUED WITH QUANTUM-BUSTING INTELLIGENCE, BUT CAN'T CONCENTRATE ON ANYTHING BUT BUILDING DAMS!

DR. THEODORE TOMLINSON-- THE SCIENCE PROFESSOR WHO CREATED THE AX-CELL-ERATOR!

I FOUND OUT IT'S, LIKE, SUPER, TOO. SUPER POWERED. UNBREAKABLE. LIKE SUPERM--

HOW DID YOU...? YOU KNOW...

I RAN IT OVER WITH MY CAR.

THAT WAS A TRYING MOMENT.

WOW, SO THE SUPER POWERS REALLY SOMETHING TO IT, HUH?

WORD, YO.

PREVIOUSLY IN FRESHMEN:

AFTER DISCOVERING THEIR BIZARRE AND AMAZING POWERS, OUR YOUNG HEROES WERE EMPLOYED BY THE CREATOR OF THE AX-CELL-ERATOR, DR. TOMLINSON, TO HELP REPAIR THE MACHINE THAT COULD CURE ALL DISEASES AND EVEN PREVENT AGING.

WANNABE, SUPERHERO OBSESSED BUT POWERLESS, TRIED TO TAKE LEADERSHIP, BUT HE WAS CONSTANTLY DISOBEYED BY HIS REBELLIOUS TEAMMATES.

THE SEDUCTRESS WAS CRITICALLY INJURED IN THE KIDS' FIRST BATTLE WITH THE MYSTERIOUSLY SUPER POWERED FRAT GUYS. AGAINST THE WISHES OF THE BEAVER AND WANNABE, THE PUPPETEER HAS JUMPED INTO HER COMATOSE MIND.

DISTRESSED THAT HIS TEAM DOES NOT RESPECT HIM AND UPSET THAT ANNALEE, HIS UNREQUITED LOVE, DISOBEYED HIM, WANNABE WAS CAPTURED BY THE FRAT GUYS FIVE DAYS AGO...

SUSIE, FOR THE LAST TIME! I CAN'T PROMISE YOU THAT I'LL NEVER WATER ANOTHER PLANT! THAT'S RIDICULOUS! IT'S NOT CHEATING!

How can you say that! You're so *insensitive!* Oh, God, three years! I've wasted three of the best years of my life on you!

SO... OKAY. FOLLOW ME HERE.

ASK YOURSELF... WHAT WOULD ALIENS THINK ABOUT THE GAME OF GOLF? YOU WALK UP TO A BALL... HIT IT AS FAR AWAY FROM YOURSELF AS YOU CAN...

AND THEN YOU WALK UP TO IT AGAIN.

WHAT THE *BLEEEP*, MAN?

I'M STARTING TO FIGURE THIS OUT, PAULA. I'M IN YOUR NEURAL NETWORK. I CAN SEE WHAT THOUGHTS YOU'RE USING.

THESE... TENTACLES... THEY'RE CONNECTING THE MEMORIES, THE EXPERIENCES OF YOUR LIFE.

THEY'RE CONSTANTLY GROWING, MAKING NEW CONNECTIONS.

THESE JUNCTIONS ARE YOUR MEMORIES. THEY'RE CREATING EMOTIONS, WHICH SPILL OUT THROUGH THE TENTACLES.

THEY MAKE CONNECTIONS WITH EACH OTHER.

HARD-WIRING YOUR EXPERIENCES TO EMOTIONS.

YOUR LOVE OF YOUR MOTHER GETS CONNECTED TO CRITICISMS OF YOUR APPEARANCE.

STOP IT, ANNALEE.

YOUR APPEARANCE IS CONNECTED TO REJECTION. THE CHEERLEADERS.

REJECTION IS CONNECTED TO SELF-LOATHING. MAKING YOURSELF SICK IN THE GYM.

AND THAT'S CONNECTED TO OVEREATING.

THE POOL BENEATH ME IS YOUR SUBCONSCIOUS. YOUR PERSONALITY, YOUR IDENTITY. YOUR *FEELING SYSTEM*.

PLEASE, ANNALEE. PLEASE STOP.

YOU'RE POISONING YOURSELF WITH YOUR OWN THOUGHTS.

THERE ARE WONDERFUL MEMORIES IN HERE, PAULA.

WHY AREN'T YOU USING THEM?

WEEE!

COME HERE, PAULA. COME INTO THIS MEMORY.

I DON'T WANT TO.

YOU HAVE TO, PAULA. I'M GOING TO MAKE YOU.

I-- I CAN'T.

YOUR FATHER IS HERE AND HE LOVES YOU.

IT'S SAFE HERE, PAULA.

I-- I DON'T...

GET IN HERE, PAULA!

NOW!

KRRAKKOOOOMM

WHAT DOES IT MATTER IF HE LOVES ME? HE'S MY FATHER!

WHAT DO YOU MEAN "WHAT DOES IT MATTER--?"

HE DOESN'T *CARE* WHAT I LOOK LIKE!

PAULA--

HE'S NOT GOING TO HAVE TO MARRY ME! HOW AM I EVER GOING TO FIND SOMEONE *ATTRACTED* TO ME?

PAULA, YOU'RE *NOT* UGLY--

BUT NOBODY IS EVER GOING TO FEEL *PASSION* ABOUT ME. NOBODY'S EVER GOING TO WALK INTO A ROOM AND SAY "OH, I NEED *THAT* GIRL. I *WANT* THAT GIRL."

YES THEY WILL--

NOT UNLESS I USE MY POWERS.

THAT'S NOT TRUE--

DON'T HAND ME THAT *BULL BLEEP*, ANNALEE. IT'S TOO EASY FOR YOU. YOU'RE MISS CUTIE PIE, PEOPLE FALL IN LOVE WITH YOU THE SECOND THEY LOOK AT YOU.

YOU HAVE TO LOVE *YOURSELF*, PAULA. YOU HAVE TO SEE YOUR OWN BEAUTY, AND THEN OTHERS WILL TOO.

LOOK-- JUST FROM BEING INSIDE THIS MEMORY FOR A MINUTE-- LOOK AT THE SKY CLEARING UP.

LOOK WHAT THE LOVE INSIDE HERE IS DOING FOR YOU. CREATING PEACE, SERENITY. SAFETY. IT'S LIKE MEDICINE FOR YOUR SOUL.

THESE BLUE TENTACLES-- I THINK THEY'RE YOUR GOOD THOUGHTS. THEY'RE SUPPOSED TO PROTECT YOU.

THEY'RE SUPPOSED TO HOLD BACK YOUR SADNESS, KEEP YOUR FEARS AT BAY. KEEP YOU HEALTHY.

BUT YOU'VE CONDITIONED YOURSELF TO *MISERY*. YOU'VE TRAINED YOUR SELF-LOATHING TO POISON YOUR EMOTIONS.

YOU'RE CREATING YOUR OWN REALITY.

AND IT'S *MISERABLE*.

YOU DON'T UNDERSTAND, ANNALEE. YOU NEVER WILL.

OH, YES, I WILL.

SOMETHING HAS BROKEN LOOSE. THERE'S SOMETHING... SOME *PAIN* THAT'S GOTTEN TOO BIG FOR YOU TO HANDLE.

PLEASE... PLEASE DON'T.

LET ME HELP YOU, PAULA. LET ME FIND IT.

TRUST IN ME, PAULA. PLEASE.

I'LL UNDERSTAND. I PROMISE. I WON'T JUDGE. LET ME HELP.

TELL ME WHAT IT IS, PAULA.

LET ME FIND IT, PAULA. STOP TRYING TO CUT ME OFF.

PLEASE STOP THIS, ANNALEE.

DON'T FIGHT ME, PAULA. I KNOW I'M CLOSE. I CAN HEAR YOUR MEMORIES FIRING, LIKE A RACING HEARTBEAT.

JUST LEAVE. I'M BEGGING YOU.

THESE MEMORIES, PAULA--THEY'RE ALL IN THE PAST. YOU CAN'T LET THEM RUIN YOUR FUTURE.

HI... UHM... PERRY? I... UHM... HI?

WHAT?

I WAS WONDERING... Y'KNOW... NO, I'M SORRY.

NO SWEAT.

I MEAN-- I'M SORRY. WOULD YOU--

WHAT IS IT?!

WELL...I WAS JUST...WONDERING...IF YOU WEREN'T DOING ANYTHING...I MEAN, IF YOU HADN'T ALREADY MADE PLANS, I MEAN, OF COURSE YOU'VE-- BUT IF YOU HADN'T ALREADY ASKED ANYONE--

OH, COME ON, PAULA. *THIS* GUY?

THIS GUY IS *SO* NOT WORTH SWEATING.

IF YOU MIGHT... CONSIDER... GOING TO THE PROM WITH ME...?

HAHAHAHA HA HAHA...

NAW, NAW, OH-- OH, YOU DIDN'T--

HAHAHAHA HA HAHA...

HOLD ON, HOLD ON--

DAVE--DAVE--YOU GOTTA-- HOLD ON, YO, HOLD ON, YOU GOTTA HEAR THIS--

OKAY, SO THIS WAS PRETTY HARSH. I CAN UNDERSTAND WHY IT HURT.

I... I... WHAT--?

BUT SERIOUSLY, PAULA. *LOOK* AT THIS KID. WHAT IS HE *REALLY* WORTH?

HE'S GOOD LOOKING, BUT THAT'S NOTHING BUT GENETIC. THAT DOESN'T MAKE A PERSON WORTH A DAMN.

TELL HIM WHAT YOU JUST SAID. GO AHEAD. PLEASE!

SERIOUSLY, YO, HE'S GOTTA HEAR THIS.

HE'S WEARING CLOTHES FROM TWO DIFFERENT SPORTS TEAMS, WHICH MEANS HE'S A COMPLETE TOOL. THE CLOTHES ARE FOR SHOW, THEY DON'T MEAN ANYTHING TO HIM. HE DOESN'T CARE ABOUT THESE TEAMS.

AND THE COCK-EYED HAT-- SUPPOSED TO CONVEY INDIFFERENCE OR WHATEVER--BUT LOOK HOW HARD HE WORKED TO GET THIS THING CROOKED-- HE HAD TO BREAK THE BRIM. THAT SOUND INDIFFERENT TO YOU?

THE PANTS TOO LOW-- FALLING OFF? PUH-LEEZE. WHAT SELF-RESPECTING PERSON WOULD INTENTIONALLY HANDICAP THEMSELVES IN SUCH A WAY SO THEY CAN'T EVEN MOVE?

FAKE JEWELRY. FAKE DETROIT ACCENT--FROM A KID WHO GOES TO SCHOOL IN NEW HAMPSHIRE?

WHAT'S GOING ON INSIDE HIS HEAD, PAULA? *THINK* ABOUT IT.

WHAT JUST--DID WE GET DISCONNECTED?

NO, MAN, HE HUNG UP. HE *BLEEEP* HUNG--

NO, WAY--HE WOULDN'T--

CLICK
BZZZZZZ...

NO, OF COURSE HE WOULDN'T...

I ZINK 'E JUST DEED.

BLEEEP WAY, MAN.

WOULD YOU JUST SHUT THE *BLEEP* UP, MAN--THE GEEK WOULDN'T DO THAT, HE'S ALL ABOUT US BEING SUPERHEROES--

YEAH, AND LOOK AT THE WAY YOU'VE BEEN TREATING HIM, *I'D* TURN ON US TOO--

OH, NICE, SO YOU JUST TURN ON YOUR FRIENDS?!

THAT'S WHAT I'M TRYING TO *TELL* YOU, YOU STUPID *BLEEP*, WE'RE NOT HIS *BLEEEP* FRIENDS!

WE'VE NEVER BEEN HIS FRIENDS.

NEXT ISSUE: FINALS!

CAST OUT OF THE MAIN DORMS AND FORCED TO LIVE IN TEMPORARY HOUSING IN THE BOUGHL SCIENCE BUILDING, THE FRESHMEN CLASS OF FREESE COLLEGE HAS BEEN IMBUED WITH MIRACULOUS SUPERPOWERS BY THE EXPLOSION OF A MYSTERIOUS DEVICE CALLED THE AX-CELL-ERATOR!

WANNABE-- KENNETH "NORRIN" WEISMEYER, THE WOULD-BE TEAM LEADER AND RESIDENT SUPERHERO GEEK, WHO WENT FOR PIZZA DURING THE PIVOTAL MOMENT AND HAS NO POWERS!

THE PUPPETEER-- ANNALEE ROGERS, WHO CAN JUMP INTO PEOPLE'S MINDS AND VIEW THEIR MEMORIES OR EVEN CONTROL THEM!

THE GREEN THUMB-- CHARLES LEVY, A DEDICATED VEGETARIAN WHO CAN NOW COMMUNICATE WITH PLANTS, LEAVING HIM NOTHING TO EAT!

QUAKER-- LIAM ADAMS, THE AMISH BOY WHO CAN CAUSE EARTHQUAKES BY SHUFFLING HIS BELLY!

THE INTOXICATOR-- ELWOOD JOHNS, FORMER MATH GENIUS WHOSE DRUNKEN BURPS INTOXICATE ANYONE WHO SMELLS THEM!

THE DRAMA TWINS-- RENEE AND BRADY, BICKERING EXES WHO MUST BE IN PHYSICAL CONTACT TO USE THEIR TELEKINESIS!

THE SQUIRREL-- JACQUES LALLEAUX, THE FRENCH EXCHANGE STUDENT WHO COMPULSIVELY HOARDS NUTS!

THE SEDUCTRESS-- PAULA POPHOUSE, THE LOVELORN TEEN WHO CAN MAKE ANYONE FALL IN LOVE WITH HER!

THE BEAVER-- THE SCHOOL MASCOT HAS BEEN IMBUED WITH QUANTUM-BUSTING INTELLIGENCE, BUT CAN'T CONCENTRATE ON ANYTHING BUT BUILDING DAMS!

DR. THEODORE TOMLINSON-- THE SCIENCE PROFESSOR WHO CREATED THE AX-CELL-ERATOR!

PREVIOUSLY IN FRESHMEN:

AFTER DISCOVERING THEIR BIZARRE AND AMAZING POWERS, OUR YOUNG HEROES WERE EMPLOYED BY THE CREATOR OF THE AX-CELL-ERATOR, DR. TOMLINSON, TO HELP REPAIR THE MACHINE THAT COULD CURE ALL DISEASES AND EVEN PREVENT AGING.

IN THE KIDS' FIRST BATTLE WITH THE SUPERPOWERED FRAT GUYS, QUAKER HESITATED TO USE HIS POWERS AND PAULA, THE SEDUCTRESS, WAS INJURED AND REMAINS IN A COMA. THE PUPPETEER JUMPED INTO PAULA'S MIND AND FOUND THAT SHE DOES NOT WANT TO WAKE UP: SHE'S WALLOWING IN SHAME BECAUSE SHE USED HER POWERS TO MAKE EXCHANGE STUDENT JACQUES (THE SQUIRREL) FALL IN LOVE WITH HER.

THE FRAT GUYS HAVE BEEN IMBUED WITH SUPER STRENGTH VIA THE ADDICTIVE TOUCH OF DR. TOMLINSON, WHO WAS ALSO AFFECTED BY THE AX-CELL-ERATOR. DR. TOMLINSON INTENDS TO PROVE HIS INVENTION TO THE WORLD BY RELEASING A CANCER-CAUSING AGENT INTO THE WATER SUPPLY AND USING THE AX-CELL-ERATOR TO CURE HIS VICTIMS.

WANNABE, SCORNED BY HIS PEERS AND HIS UNREQUITED LOVE, ANNALEE, HAS TURNED AGAINST HIS TEAM AND JOINED DR. TOMLINSON IN HIS QUEST TO BECOME A SUPERHERO...

PAULA, NO!

FRESHMEN

INTRODUCTION TO SUPERPOWERS 106: FINALS!

THE POINT I'M GETTING AT IS THAT THIS GROUP OF HUMAN CHILDREN I'VE TAKEN ON...

...I DON'T KNOW IF THEY HAVE THE HEART TO STOP THIS EVIL WHICH ATTEMPTS TO PASS.

Acknowledgements

A lot of my friends rallied to help me on this project. Beside my best friend, there were Dan Milano and Matthew Huffman, who helped us create the characters. Matt Senreich told Top Cow to call me for some good comic ideas. On a separate occasion, Freddie Prinze and Conrad Jackson fearlessly did the same thing. Matt also asked Cartoon Network to air our ads during Robot Chicken, and he and Geoff Johns sat down with me to offer advice about the comic industry. Geoff, Sarah Michelle Gellar, Mila Kunis and Joss Whedon all lent their names to profoundly indifferent cover quotes—Mila even offered her likeness as the Puppeteer, and pimped us to Stuff Magazine. Cat, from DJ's Universal Comics in Studio City, picked me up every time I walked in his store. On the Internet, a host of unbelievably loyal fans welcomed me daily, sometimes with photos of them dressed as our characters. Mark Piccirilli moderated the forum very smoothly. My cousin Ben and my most beloved friend, Derek, both of whom I miss dearly, tirelessly believed in me and left their spirits in my heart. Both this work and my life are dedicated to them. Bill, my most trusted pal, kept me calm. Fat Buddy licked me. My dad, Poppa Sterb, brought our posters to his local comic book stores. And the lovely Lisa, who will be my bride just days after this is printed, is the greatest co-pilot this imaginative guy could imagine.

As represented on the page, the astounding Leonard Kirk created relentlessly brilliant visuals, somehow shoehorning my dense story onto the page. Andrew Pepoy's inks brought him home flawlessly, while the phenomenal Troy Peteri worked overtime to squeeze the Drama Twins' dense dialogue into those unforgiving panels, and Tyson Wengler always kept the Beaver brown. Rodolfo Migliari's covers progressed from jaw-dropping to worthy of weeping. Jim McLauchlin tried (valiantly) to keep my neuroses under control, while Matt Hawkins, Renae Geerlings, Scott Tucker and Annie Pham did all the real work.

And then there's my best friend, who all of you know as the Big Famous Actor. He's the one who everybody asks about, the one who needs security, the one with the busy schedule and the nicknames and the tireless publicist, Brenda, and the awesome manager, Trice. He's the one who was on Buffy, the one who stole The Italian Job, the one you need to ask about Austin Powers 4 or compliment on Party Monster. That's all true. But then there's the guy I know: My internal enemy's worst enemy. My truest true believer. The one who makes me feel like the star. I'd tell you about him, but it's a secret.

-Hugh

Freshmen Yearbook!

Cacophony by Shawn Dubin and Tyson Wengler
Seductress by J. Michael Linsner and Steve Firchow
Wannabe by Leonard Kirk and Blond
Puppeteer by Randy Green and Tyson Wengler
Intoxicator by Bill Sienkiewicz and Blond
The Beaver by Scott Benefiel and Blond
Drama Twins by Nathan Cabrera
Professor and Frat Guys by Keu Cha
The Squirrel by Tyler Kirkham and Blond
Green Thumb by Rodolfo Migliari and Blond
Quaker by Tone Rodriguez and Blond
Long Dong by Howard Chaykin and Michelle Madsen

ADVENTURE, EXCITEMENT. A FRESHMAN CRAVES NOT THESE THINGS.

CACOPHONY

Lisa Rohr named herself Cacophony in seventh grade, when she became the lead singer of a punk band she put together with the other kids in her low-income project. "Benny the Hook," as they called themselves, entertained the other kids in the projects playing whatever abandoned musical instruments they could find or make. Eventually, the adults forced them to stop their noise.

As an orphan living with a mentally disturbed aunt who could barely put food on the table, Cacophony became a scrapper and a loner, and most people found her constant glaring off-putting. When she was accepted to D.W. Freese College on a music scholarship, she took the opportunity to attend mostly for assurance that she'd have meals for four years in the dining halls.

When the Ax-Cell-Erator exploded, Cacophony was given the power to recreate any sound with her voice. She can make herself sound like an entire orchestra once she hears their music. She left the school immediately and headed to Los Angeles, where she is competing in a reality TV singing competition and resisting the advances of one of the judges. She has been seen at public events with actor Seth Green, but neither will comment on their relationship.

LINSNER
POST - MARILYN

Raised by a wealthy family in New Hampshire, Paula Pophouse was expected to be an upwardly mobile socialite. But when her contractor father passed away unexpectedly, everything changed. Paula was left in the care of her shallow mother, who was ill-prepared for a close, caring relationship with a troubled young girl.

Paula lost herself in romance novels and movies, becoming obsessive about classic and modern Hollywood couples and dreaming of one day finding her knight in shining armor. But she constantly struggled with her self-image, losing herself to her own superficial perceptions of how people are supposed to look. Paula battled eating binges and daily workouts and dug her self-esteem a very early grave.

As The Seductress, Paula is able to make anyone fall in love with her. It's her lifelong wish come true, but it's also far too easy a power to abuse for such a young, impressionable girl with an unquenchable, lifelong thirst for affection. She has enraptured the exchange student, Jacques. At first, it was revenge for his sug-gestion that she call herself "Beer Goggles." But now she's falling madly in love with him, despite her fear that this relationship will end terribly if anyone finds out what she's done.

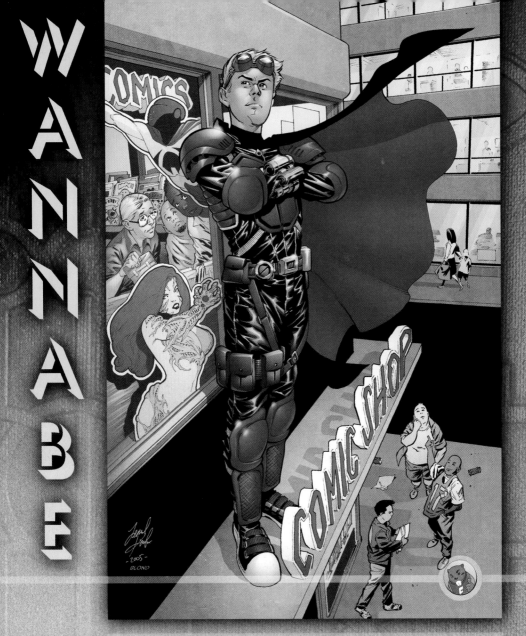

WANNABE

Kenneth Weismeyer never discovered a love for comic books—it was born with him. His father taught him to read from the classic adventures of the silver age, and soon he was bagging and boarding and trolling a paper route to pay for his weekly addiction. He dubbed himself "Norrin" after his favorite comic book hero, also an outcast, and took to broadcasting his proud geekhood with stickers, T–shirts and hats.

Norrin's middle-class upbringing outside Pittsburgh was frustratingly uneventful. The son of a steelworker and a dog trainer, Norrin dreamed of a bigger future—a calling that would cast him into the role of hero. For a short time he thought he was the target of a secret hoax where he was transplanted to another dimension and everyone around him was an alien performing as his acquaintance. And then there was a month-long excavation in the woods behind his house, where he was sure evil aliens had begun burrowing to the Earth's core.

Older, wiser, but no less a comic fan, Norrin attended Freese College hoping to raise his grades and transfer to USC for film school. He'd put his dreams of adventure behind him, until his fellow students housed in the science building were infused with superpowers upon the explosion of the Ax-Cell-Erator. Finally answering the call of duty, Norrin has taken his self-imposed mantle of leadership very seriously. He has constructed a suit of armor and various comic-inspired weapons, planning to strike fear in the heart of villains everywhere... but one of his first moves was to break his own nose with his grappling hook launcher. He hopes to somehow gain the respect of his hostile teammates, who simply won't take their calling seriously, and his unrequited love, Annalee.

Annalee Rogers was a fun-loving girl until her parents' very ugly divorce during her junior year of high school, when she became introverted and introspective. The constant counseling hasn't helped—in fact, it has hasn't served any purpose other than to make her parents feel like they can wash their hands of guilt. Annalee wasn't against the idea of therapy, she just thought the people her parents hired were low-grade putzes who couldn't really understand her.

As high school progressed and her friends became involved in dramatic and toxic relationships that routinely shattered their emotions and paralyzed their intellect, she became more interested in the subject of counseling and decided to pursue psychology at college. And, again, as soon as she arrived, she was stunned and confused by the way the other kids constructed their own emotional and social roadblocks. And yet, she was still unable to divorce herself from what she considered stupid, childish conventions—like crushes on cute frat guys.

When the Ax-Cell-Erator exploded, Annalee became The Puppeteer. She is able to jump into people's minds for a few minutes at a time—far longer if they're unconscious—and sift through their memories or even control their bodies. Her own body is a completely defenseless shell while she's using her powers, though, and any damage she inflicts on her host body also appears on her own. She's voice of reason on the Freshmen team, and has just begun a journey of discovery that will take her to an understanding of the human condition that no one has ever experienced.

INTOXICATOR

Elwood Johns was a math genius from a long line of math geniuses. His father and mother, both MIT graduates, work in the pharmaceutical research industry. His brother is in Budapest studying ancient cultures on a semester-long break from Harvard. Elwood, more interested in the aerospace industry, hoped to work for NASA. He was also passionate about finance and Wall Street, voraciously reading books on the subject.

And then Elwood took his first alcoholic drink of his life, right at the pivotal moment when the Ax-Cell-Erator exploded. Now, whenever Elwood is under the influence, he produces toxic burps. Upon inhaling these ditties of doom, anyone in Elwood's vicinity becomes as intoxicated as well. His power is even more fearsome when he's hung over, because nothing stops an opponent dead faster than the immediate compulsion to retch. Elwood's personal goal has swiftly gone from working for NASA to going an entire 24 hours without throwing up. In fact, he's failing every single class he's taking.

With the help of Paula, Elwood has assembled his "coat of a thousand highs," which contains all the armament he'll need for even the most massive of battles: Flasks, cans of beers and enough joints to resurrect Miami Vice. Elwood truly is a walking machine of intoxication… but how in the world can you maintain your academic pursuits and prepare for a future in NASA when you're always hung over from being a super-hero?

Much mystery surrounds the smallest member of the Freshmen team. Captured at the age of three by a pet store with a special request from D.W. Freese College, the Beaver has spent most of his life in captivity while dreaming of freedom and building dams. He has become institutionalized—comfortable with his school sweatshirt and cushy accommodations, but is still determined to make his mark on the world of dam building.

Before ending up in the Boughl Science Building on the fateful night of the Ax-Cell-Erator's explosion, the Beaver had been captured from his cage in Freese College's athletic department and kept in the Alpha Chi Rho Frat House for six days, sustaining on a strange diet of cupcakes, Ramen Noodles, pizza and beer. He expected the worst when he was left in Paula's closet, and his fears were realized when she started screaming the moment she saw him. As he himself put it later, he was wishing he could convey to each of the kids the "astounding profundity of [their] bankrupt intelligence" when the Ax-Cell-Erator exploded, providing him with off-the-charts intelligence and a snooty English accent that matches his will to insult the students at every opportunity.

The Beaver's first and foremost love, building dams, is always present in his thoughts and dialogue. But now the Beaver leads the Freshmen (or, as he calls them, "the mongoloids") and provides them with an intelligent point of view that is often dismissive but rarely emotional.

DRAMA TWINS

When he turned 14, Brady Lee moved in with his grandmother in New Jersey. He started taking the bus to the local upper-class, snotty junior high school, where he met another outcast, the trash-talking, mafia princess, hurricane slut Renee Bellochio. It was love at first sight, and the two have been inseparable ever since. As a result, Brady has suffered two broken noses, three venereal diseases, two wrecked motorcycles and one trashed science project.

Unable to escape his obsession with this girl, Brady followed Renee to Freese College even though he wasn't enrolled. They had been fighting even more than usual, and Brady gets a pit in his stomach whenever she's out of his sight because she's so prone to cheating on him. The conflict continued once they got to school, but a brief tryst in the girls' dorm room closet during the explosion of the Ax-Cell-Erator led to Renee and Brady sharing telekinetic powers.

When they're in contact, Renee has the ability to psychically pull things toward them, while Brady can push objects away. They must work together to manipulate objects with any degree of precision, but their constant bickering hardly lends itself to cooperation. The situation is bound to reach a boiling point eventually, but for now the entire Freshmen team is trying to handle their volatility.

Doctor Theodore Tomlinson has a dream. No, an obsession. A project he has worked on for more than 40 years. And after all this time… all of the failed experiments, the mind-boggling problems, the desperate pleading for funding, the endless research and the brutal determination have paid off: The Ax-Cell-Erator is a reality.

The Ax-Cell-Erator is a breakthrough machine that irradiates cells with new, more intelligent operating instructions: Cure whatever ills them. When the Ax-Cell-Erator, still in Alpha version, exploded in the Boughl Science Building, it infused the Freshmen with superpowers based on whatever they perceived to be their biggest problem at that moment.

The Ax-Cell-Erator was destroyed in the explosion, however, and Dr. Tomlinson's funding has run out. He's determined—at any cost—to prove to the world the value of his life's work. Even if the Freshmen won't help, Dr. Tomlinson cannot allow the Ax-Cell-Erator project to die without being seen.

Meanwhile, Rob, the leader of the Alpha Chi Rho fraternity, and his fellow frat brothers, who terrorized the freshmen when they got to college and sent them into an emotional spiral the evening of the Ax-Cell-Erator's explosion, have mysterious powers as well: Jacked-up strength that seems to have no limits. And Doctor Tomlinson may have a connection with them. Time will tell…

THE SQUIRREL

Jacque Lalleaux was born to a fashion designer mother and jeweler father in the south of France. Raised as elite society from infancy, Jacques has never wanted anything in his life. With an interest in pursuing new sexual conquests in America (he's either had every woman in France or has determined them to be unworthy), Jacques arrived at Freese College and expected to rule the school. At first, everything went according to plan. Jacques bedded his orientation leader in the woman's bathroom of the Physical Therapy building, and then, later that night, a waitress at the local pizza shop. And the stewardess from his flight, also a conquest, was leaving messages on his cell phone.

But the explosion of the Ax-Cell-Erator was ill-timed for Jacques, since it came just at a moment when he was frightened by a squirrel just outside the dorm room window. Since that event, Jacques has been compulsively hoarding acorns, whenever he can get them before the wily squirrels on the Freese campus. His hair has transformed, no matter how much gel he puts into it. And lately he's seen other squirrels staring at him…

After the explosion, Jacques struck up a new relationship. He fell madly in love with Paula Pophouse, despite a complete lack of physical attraction. Since Paula's injury in the battle with the frat guys broke her spell, however, Jacques has realized that Paula used her powers on him and forced him to love her. Now Jacques is trying to come to grips with his humiliating transformation and the realization that his emotions have been manipulated at the deepest level.

Charles Levy became interested in animal protection and environmental activism when he was in sixth grade. His parents, respected Philadelphia lawyers, believed in encouraging their sons' interests and supported him in every way possible. The entire family went vegetarian, and Mr. Levy funded trips to Washington so Charles could participate in important protests. Charles even spoke in front of congress when he was only 12 years old, urging greater legislation for animal rights. This is a young man who takes himself and his work very seriously.

Although Charles has an entire greenhouse full of gorgeous, beloved plants at home in Manayunk, Pennsylvania, he chose to bring only his favorite with him to school: his Ficus Tree, which he calls Susie. He regularly speaks to Susie—a ritual recommended by an herbalist mentor of Chares', who supposes that plants can feel positive and negative reinforcements from our voices through the reverberations—and has come to think of her as the ear of his life's journal. The Ax-Cell-Erator exploded as he was whispering to her, and, when he awoke, he could hear her—and every other plant—talking.

Charles wasn't prepared for the surprisingly abrasive and negative disposition of most plants. Embittered from being displaced and potted, as well as humanity's disregard for the planet's air quality, they're very eager to tell our race's first plant whisperer what they think of us. As a result, Charles finds himself under constant attack. He's also hungry, since now most of his food can beg for mercy. And he's tired, because Susie spends all night with rampaging emotions as she repeatedly declares her love for him, but worries that he's cheating with other plants. Who knows what the future holds for Charles and his tenuous love affair with a Ficus tree…

QUAKER

Liam Adams had never left his home in Lancaster, Pennsylvania's Amish Country, before he came to Freese College. He led a very insulated life with his large family, and was quite fulfilled. Then, one night, Liam had a vision. He's unsure whether he was asleep or awake, but a great light outside his window called to him, and he was instilled with a great sensation that he had to explore beyond his hometown. The next morning, he decided that God had compelled him to go forward. Frightened and unsure, and not even completely confident in this vision, he forged ahead, and talked his parents into allowing him to go to an "English" college.

Liam is very naïve, even by Amish standards, but he knows this about himself and tries to keep quiet so he can observe rather than seem foolish. But the outrageous and often confusing machines of the outside world overwhelm and amuse him to no end.

Overweight since he was very young due to a medical condition, Liam was considering his weight when the Ax-Cell-Erator exploded. Soon after, he discovered he could make the ground shake with a roll of his ample belly. But what purpose would this serve in God's eyes? How would he be judged? How can he use this ability to serve God? Liam continues to struggle with these questions as he internalizes his guilt over Paula's injury, which he did nothing to stop out of fear for hurting Rob and the Frat Guys. More than any of the other Freshmen, Liam is alone and confused, and hoping to find a direction for himself and his new powers.

Ray McFarland has always had self-esteem problems. He was a fourth-stringer on the high school baseball team, cut from the junior varsity bowling team, rejected from the school newspaper and couldn't get a date to the senior prom. Determined to reinvent himself, Ray spent the summer between high school and college delving into pop culture, immersing himself in whatever was important to people, trying to become more viable in a college conversation. Leaving home in South Carolina for the distant Freese College, with no familiar faces to betray his life as an outcast, Ray was sure this was his big chance to change his life.

Ray already knew which fraternity he'd pledge at Freese: Alpha Chi Rho. It's where he wanted to be, with the cool kids. When he was invited to a party at their house, he jumped at the opportunity to meet some of the brothers, so they'd remember him next semester when he could pledge. He thought he was doing well, chatting up a couple of the guys, when someone suddenly grabbed and gagged him, then ripped down his pants and slung him over the balcony. Ending his dreams of being one of the cool kids. Again.

Ray was humiliated even further when some of the laughing partygoers pointed out his humble private part. Trying to figure out where he stood if five inches was indeed average, Ray was measuring himself when the Ax-Cell-Erator exploded.

Now it's fifteen feet long. And, as Ray is soon to find out, indestructible.

Watch out, world. Be on guard, ladies. Long Dong is here.

Captain's Log: The Journal of Norrin Weismeyer

Stardate: December 19th — 2pm

LAST DAY OF SCHOOL

I got B's in Intro to Film and History of Photography, A's in Creative Writing and Basic Drawing, and an A- in Sociology 101. Poor Elwood failed two of his classes. They told him he's on academic probation. If he doesn't get a 3.0 next semester, he'll be kicked out. I won't let that happen, though.

It's been a week since Paula woke up, and most of it was taken up by cramming for finals. I'm glad it's over. The week was tense. Nobody is mad at me—at least, they're not showing it if they are—but I'm mad at myself. Looking back on it, I don't know exactly where I went wrong. I may never know. But I have to learn to evaluate myself better. I have to act more like a Patrick Stewart character.

The Beaver is coming home with me for Christmas vacation—he said he needs a place to stay and wants to see Pittsburgh, but I think he wants to keep an eye on me. I hate being patronized.

The powers that Dr. Tomlinson gave me faded quickly, but they left behind an intense craving—maybe a physical addiction. I had a rough couple days getting over them, and I just wasn't up for keeping my journal. It hurt. A lot.

But it got my head in the right place. I'm turning over a new leaf. I'm becoming what I promised myself I could be. When we get back next semester, I'm going to show everybody why I should be the team's leader. And I'm going to start right now.

Mom is here to pick me up. It's an eight-hour drive to Pittsburgh (the Beaver will have to stay in a cage), and I'm going to hear all about her dog training and dad's gripes at the steel mill. And they said something about Vickie having a new boyfriend. Yuck.

Stardate: December 19th – 6pm

Mom keeps talking to the other cars. Why wouldn't they let me fly? I hate country music. Looks like the Beaver hates it even more—he's been whimpering. I need a code name—still haven't been able to come up with anything that sounds authoritative and regal. Maybe The Authority? This trip is taking forever.

Stardate: December 20th -- 12:09 am

The Beaver said something about hating humanity and disappeared into the woods, so I'm going to sleep. Mom has like 20 dogs downstairs from her boarding business. It sounds like a zoo. It smells like one of them got in my bedroom and pissed somewhere. And I think Vickie went through some of my action figures. But it's nice to have my own room to myself. In some ways, college seems like a dream that I just woke up from. Did it all really happen?

Code names: Vector? Valor? Anything other than Wannabe, that's awful. What would Stan Lee think of a hero called Wannabe?

Stardate: December 20th – 11:30 am

Weird dreams, and I slept later than I intended. Today is my first day of training. I'm going to become an idea, a legend. I'm going to strike fear into the hearts of my enemies, and inspire others to change their lives. Maybe The Captain?

Stardate: December 20th – 2:45 pm

I'm up to 25 push-ups at a time now, and I've done 1,000 crunches today. I have to go online to get some meditation training exercises, but Vickie is on the computer (she's talking on the phone, but pretending to use the computer just so I can't have it). I called and the next Tae Kwan Do class is Thursday night.

Stardate: December 20th – 7:30 pm

I have to find my Center, my Inner Self. My Northern Star.

Stardate: December 21st – 3:28 pm

I THINK MY SISTER IS DATING A SUPERVILLAIN!!!!!!

Vickie has this new boyfriend—Stang is his name (!), and apparently he's been hanging around the house a lot. Mom and Dad really like him. But Dad always said he doesn't want Vickie to date until she's 19! And Mom cooked brisket for him—she never cooks brisket when I ask for it! Something is going on, this guy has totally mesmerized my family. I felt like he was staring at me, too—trying to make eye contact or something. I kept my gaze averted, and my spirit alert.

Stardate: December 23 – 4:52 pm

Haven't written in a while, been busy. Stang (it's short for Mustang, his father is a car freak) was over again and, yet again, my family's disposition totally changed with him around. I excused myself from the dinner table—said I wasn't feeling well—and suited up. It felt good to wear the costume again, it felt right. I wonder if that's what righteous means. Anyway—

I followed Stang to his house. His family is really rich. I don't know what they do, but their property is huge. It had that weird smell, too, that smell I noticed behind the house last year when we were visited by aliens (yeah, I've started to think it was real again, I'll write more about it later).

I took notes in my pocket recorder as I looked around the house. I'll transcribe them and do analysis later. Nothing overtly diabolical to the naked eye, but that doesn't really mean anything. Stang is up to no good—he has some sort of preternatural control over my family, and I'll get to the heart of it.

Stardate: December 24th – 2:30

More weird dreams. I'm a little kid in them. Really strange. Dad went to DJ's Comics and picked up all of my pull books from the whole semester!! I forgot to tell him I found a store near school—now I have some doubles, but it's still cool. It was nice of him, because he has the truck all day and by the time he gets home, they're closed. I've been dying to read these.

Stardate: December 25th – 8 am

MERRY CHRISTMAS!!!

I got a new laptop computer! I have to get some serious security protocols going if this is going to be the keeper of the team's important data. First up: Villain profiling. Stang is coming over for "brunch." More on that later. Man, the name thing is kicking my ass. It seems like all the good names are taken. I thought about "Hardwired" now that I have a new computer. I've done 1,000 sit-ups every day, and I'm now up to 30 consecutive push-ups. I have to learn stealth.

Stardate: December 27th – 3:21 am

DISASTER!!!

I am SO PISSED OFF RIGHT NOW!!!! Stang came over for lunch and I saw him mesmerize my mom right in front of me. She completely changed her entire disposition just because he gave her this casual sideways glance. So I went upstairs and listened, and waited for him to leave.

I followed him home—which was really hard to do because he has a car and I was on my bike, and (of course) that's the minute the Beaver picks to show back up. He said he was building a dam—I don't even wanna know where he built it or whether it's gonna cause any irrigation problems in the woods (Irrigation? Right word?). So he wants to know what I'm doing, and I tell him, and he flips out and tells me I'm being a mongoloid. We had this huge fight, which was really frustrating because I don't understand half the things he says, and I got angry and left for Stang's house. I took the shortcut through McGready's farm (turns out he's not really a Chupacabra after all—gotta write more about that).

So I get to Stang's house and find his garage door slightly open. I knew it was the perfect opportunity for an entrance, so I slid under. I ripped my cape a little bit, but I got in undetected. His house is huge! They have Xbox 360! Stang and his older brother sat down to play Call of Duty, so I used my stealth skills to sneak into his room. He has pictures of girls all over the walls—Vickie won't like it when she sees that. I heard someone coming, so I hid in his closet. There was plenty of room in there, and I covered up with some stuff on the floor. I practiced my meditation, having the forethought to know I might be stuck there until morning. The door opened, and I reached into my Inner Self to slow my heartbeat and breathing, making myself undetectable—

—and it was the Beaver!!!

(I recorded this dialogue on my gauntlet's digital voice recorder, for future reference in case he tries to misrepresent this moment).

"Norrin, have you completely lost your woefully precarious grasp on sanity?"

"What? No—shut up, I'm on a stakeout!"

"You're concealed in this dimwitted club foot's closet, buried beneath mounds of soiled clothing—wearing a cape, no less—and—"

"Shut up! They're going to hear you!"

"Perhaps you should seek psychological counseling, Norrin. You're simply too prone to overblown speculations which lead to flights of absurd extravagance."

"He has mesmerized my family!"

The Beaver stared at me for a moment, mouth agape, moving his nose up and down. Those stupid teeth seemed to be mocking me.

"Have you gone completely and utterly off the proverbial deep end? What are you doing for the future of your race? What possible asset are you to society?"

I'd had enough. "If he has a mind control device, I have to find out about it!"

"A mind... control... device? On the shoulders of your forefathers, under the weight of their blood, sweat and tears, you mount this declaration of intellectual nihilism?"

And then the door opened.

And the Beaver and I looked up at Stang. Blankly and dumbly.

I would have thought of this, but the Beaver kicked on my ultrabright headlight, temporarily blinding Stang. He pushed me out of the closet and we raced down the stairs. Stang's parents must have been sleeping, because I heard them respond to his yelling. The brother never put down the Xbox 360 controller.

We got out of the house and now I'm home. I catalogued all the details I could remember about Stang's house and his room into the Villain Database, but I don't have enough raw data to run a composite just yet. The Beaver has been lecturing me nonstop. I'm trying to make him understand that it's better to be safe than sorry—that if we'd done our homework on Dr. Tomlinson, we would have known not to help him reassemble the Ax-Cell-Erator, and it's likely that Paula would never have gotten hurt (by the way, the Beaver called Annalee and it turns out that Paula has movement in her arms and legs, she's going to be fine).

Stardate: December 27th - 4:11 am
The Beaver still hasn't stopped talking. He just compared me to Napoleon, James Cameron and Charles Lindbergh.

Stardate: December 30th – 2:45 pm
The Beaver won't let me out of his sight. Even when I try to leave him behind, he just follows. Mom thinks he's adorable. I'm up to 35 push-ups at a time. I've definitely put on some muscle. Tae Kwon Do class went great. More weird dreams, by the way—could someone in the area have a dream control device?

Stardate: January 3rd, 4:25 pm

Stang was just over and the Beaver observed him. He says he's a "charmer." He says humans act silly and stupid around people they like, and my family likes Stang. I know what a charmer is, I just don't find Stang all that charming. Sounds fishy to me. Still, though, I understand what he's saying. I keep wondering how Annalee's vacation is going.

Stang doesn't seem to remember what happened, or at least he hasn't said anything about it to us. There's no way he could have known it was me, the costume and goggles conceal my identity very nicely.

45 push-ups a day now, and 2,000 sit-ups. I've started weightlifting on days when I don't have Tae Kwon Do, and it's going really well. The Beaver is watching my every move. He's driving me nuts. Only 10 more days until I go back to Freese.

Stardate: January 4th – 4:38 am

The Beaver is cuddled up on one of my sister's stuffed bears—it really doesn't look right. I've seen him have some really intense sessions with Paula's bunny slippers at school, too. I think he needs a girl.

Anyway, I got woken up by that dream again and I wanted to write it down while I remembered it. I've been seeing this guy who looked really familiar, and it just struck me.

His name is Mr. Fiddlesticks, and he's from this children's book I had when I was a little kid—"Mr. Fiddlesticks goes to Africa." It was a whole series, but I didn't have any of the other books. At first I could just sort of hear him talking in my dream. Then I saw him a couple times, sort of really weird, like he was kind of there and kind of not there. It's hard to explain. Tonight was really different, though—I felt like he was talking to me. I actually felt like he was really here. He's very tall and thin, and annoyingly polite and proper—like a friendly version of the Beaver. He always knew all of the customs in other countries, and he'd teach them to kids in his books. He warned me that danger is coming, and I need to be prepared for it.

Like I didn't know that!

Something else happened, though, more importantly! Right when I woke up, it hit me, just like I knew it would—perfectly square in the gut. An answer out of the blue, like a calling from above: My code name! Henceforth, I shall be known as The Scarlet Knight! And I shall cast fear into the heart of villains with my Scarlet Armory. And track them with my Scarlet Computer!

The ~~dawn~~ dusk of the Scarlet Knight is upon us!

Man, the Beaver really should get a room with that stuffed bear.

That's all for this journal. Tomorrow, I'll begin The Chronicles of the Scarlet Knight! Excelsior!

FRESHMEN

Cover Gallery

Freshmen issue #1 clockwise from top left:
art by: **Joseph Michael Linsner**
art by: **George Perez** and **Tyson Wengler**
(above and to the left) art by: **Rodolfo Migliari, the pride of Argentina**

Freshmen issue #2
art by: Rodolfo Migliari

concept art shown left

Freshmen issue #3
art by: Rodolfo Migliari

concept art shown right

Freshmen issue #4
art by: Rodolfo Migliari

concept art shown left

Freshmen issue #5
art by: Rodolfo Migliari

concept art shown right

after John Buscema

Shown above

Freshmen issue #6
art by: Rodolfo Migliari

facing page top

Freshmen: Yearbook
art by: Rodolfo Migliari
art by: Leonard Kirk and Kevin Senft with
design by Zach Matheny

Freshmen Holiday Card
art by: Rodolfo Migliari

Happy
Holidays!

shown above, character designs by
Leonard Kirk

and below, cover concepts for *Freshmen* issue #1 variants by
Joseph Michael Linsner

Freshmen II: The Fundamentals of Fear

trade paperback vol.2

created by:
Seth Green and **Hugh Sterbakov**

written by:
Hugh Sterbakov

pencils by:
Randy Green, Will Conrad and
Jorge Correa

Collects *Freshmen* vol. 2 issues #1 - #6. Led by a lifelong comic book fan who missed the life-changing event that gave the kids their superpowers, the team faces a new mystery in the form of a missing student, a new villain that haunts their darkest fears and a cataclysmic rift within their ranks in the most anticipated sequel of all time, *Freshmen II: Fundamentals of Fear!* This edition also features an all new bonus story by writer Hugh Sterbakov!

"Freshmen II? Why isn't is called sophomores?"

–Sarah Michelle Gellar

(ISBN 13: 978-1-58240-732-6) US $16.99

volume 1
collects issues #80-#85
(ISBN 13: 978-1-58240-906-1)
U.S.D. $9.99

volume 2
collects issues #86-#92
(ISBN 13: 978-1-58240-886-6)
U.S.D. $14.99

volume 3
collects issues #93-#100
(ISBN 13: 978-1-58240-887-3)
U.S.D. $14.99

Witchbalde

volume 1 - volume 3

written by: **Ron Marz**
pencils by: **Mike Choi, Stephen Sadowski, Keu Cha,
Chris Bachalo** and more!

Get in on the ground floor of Top Cow's flagship title with these affordable trade paperback collections from Ron Marz's series re-defining run on *Witchblade*! Each volume collects a key story arc in the continuing adventures of Sara Pezzini and the Witchblade.

Also available from Top Cow Productions, Inc.